LITANIES NEAR WATER

poems

Litanies Near Water

PAULA CLOSSON BUCK

LOUISIANA STATE UNIVERSITY PRESS
BATON ROUGE

Published by Louisiana State University Press

Manufactured in the United States of America

An LSU Press Paperback Original
First printing

Designer: Michelle A. Neustrom
Typeface: Warnock Pro
Printer and binder: Thomson-Shore, Inc.

Library of Congress Cataloging-in-Publication Data

Buck, Paula Closson, 1957–
Litanies near water : poems / Paula Closson Buck.
p. cm.
"An LSU Press paperback original"—T.p. verso.
ISBN-13: 978-0-8071-3297-5 (pbk. : alk. paper)
I. Title.
PS3552.U3339L58 2008
811'.6—dc22
2007019758

The author acknowledges, with thanks, the editors of the following journals, in which poems or versions of poems from *Litanies Near Water* first appeared: *Agni:* "Litany of Resistance," "Report from the Aftermath," "Report from the Compound," "Report from My Own Backyard," and "Tigers"; *Agni* online: "Landscape with a Very Fat Man, Seated" and "What They Had Come For"; *Basalt:* "Primer in Black" and "Verona as the Past"; *Denver Quarterly:* "Last Days," "Metaphor as Prayer," "A Mother's Ten-Second History Lesson," and "Waiting for Tassos"; *Gettysburg Review:* "Beetle," "If Silence Is Any Indication," "The Moment: Stone Fish," "Night in Venice: Summer," "November Consolation," and "Theory of an Impersonal God"; *Laurel Review:* "Elegy for My Novel," "The Heart Is," "Monk Killed by Tractor in Bid to Dodge Police," and "The Smallest Man Carries the Candle"; *Ohio Review:* "After the Feast" and "You Cannot Love the Wind"; *Shenandoah:* "Pagan Litany"; and *Southern Review:* "Confessions of the Natural World."

Thanks also to the Pennsylvania Council on the Arts for a grant that made the beginnings of this book possible.

The paper in this book meets the guidelines for permanence and durability of the Committee on Production Guidelines for Book Longevity of the Council on Library Resources. ♾

for Jim and Conrad,
my partners in this adventure

Contents

I

THE SMALLEST MAN CARRIES THE CANDLE

IF SILENCE IS ANY INDICATION

then one night the muse went down to the river
with the patriarchal God. Together
they went, Big G, little maker of odes.
The carp slept. The flag flagged
on the riverbank. And they . . .

well at first, of course, swam
almost as if they were lovers, or a pair
of otters; they dove and wallowed on their backs.

Had you been there, you'd have thought
that you'd been there before,
and so would have known that laughter
is followed by its absence—
their laughter, rippling like neon on the oily back
of the river as they negotiated
the muck of the bottom,
to be followed by their absence.

Whose idea to hold each other under?
That old inquisitorial trick for getting the magic out.
God's beard rippled, dictatorial as a weed.
The muse—not as strong, but a better swimmer—
turned effervescent, pale bubbles rising from a face
still stubborn with secrets.

And who do you think
could hold breath longer?—
his hand on her head (not in blessing),
her hand on his.

NOVEMBER CONSOLATION

Katerina is crying
and no one can make her stop.
She wanted Turkish candy,
or yogurt with honey—
she is tired or injured or sad.

More generally speaking, it is November—
a time of wooden tables and men in cafés,
Americans on TV threatening war.
The world undertakes
its oversized grief.

In the olive grove behind Katerina's
and the house where I stay, two exfoliated hens
nest on a cushion in the dirt.

They always welcome a fugitive
from the massive
scale on which things take place.

This village collapses
one uninhabited room at a time.
And each day arrives
like a perfect egg. Or two.
There there, Katerina.

THE SMALLEST MAN CARRIES THE CANDLE

Feast of Aghia Varvara, December 2002

The concrete skeletons of holiday houses
damage the landscape. A coal-gray sea
rolls in. The chant of the priest

snags and wavers, runs its hagiography through us
like a tape in a player whose batteries are dying.
Women cross themselves, pat their breasts.

The smallest man carries the candle.
Then it's fish and chickpeas all around,
chickpeas and cabbage and sweets.

I drink rakí, speak English into the bad ear
of the chief of police—lightly,
since my tourist visa's lapsed. Down the road

past winter-greened hillsides,
thirty Iraqi refugees saved from drowning
lean from the windows of a municipal building.

I've no more right to be here, but the chief
is a good man—a hand-shaking, well-wishing
man—so kind he makes me want to say

I'm no accomplice in their misery either.
And haven't I drunk to the beautiful martyr,
haven't I paid

for the doves to sit atop these dovecotes
burbling and smoothing white feathers
like glossy advertisements for peace?

YOU CANNOT LOVE THE WIND

It is not like a first wife
you delete with a thick, black stroke
or the memory of her irritating habits.
It is not the lover you leave her for, carrying
only your suitcase. You congratulate yourself years later.
But the wind reduces you to stubborn
little steps, forces you to bend slightly
against the invisible.
                                        The wind sweeps
sand at the tender skin of your legs,
into your face with the sting of insult
you know must be true.
It takes from you even your curses.

Seal your lips and cover your head.
Close the shutters and lock the door.
Arrange your hair; please yourself

with this stillness. Yours is the little death
the wind will not grieve over.

Not for you the hysterical figs,
the olive trees beating their breasts
outside your window, fruitless pistachios
going through the motions of an arbitrary, obstinate

howl. Whatever you are, the wind will have forgotten you
long before you know anything of love.

REPORT FROM THE COMPOUND

All night the guard's whistle
peeps like a Brink's frog
at the perimeter

All is well, all is well. Danger's
not a headline, but a pulse.
Behind the T-shirt cooperative,

the horses have taken up
their feud with the dogs
while inside, cotton torsos,

at rest from the optimism
of women, await
the rapid fire

of sewing machines.
The frogs have taken over
the green pool

where we wash and swim.
Haven't we held them,
admiring the pale

pucker of their throats?
They are not the dead lovers
of Gioconda Belli,

that tragic Sandinista.
They keep on, as steady
and inexhaustible

as accountants.
For every man shot
at close range,

there's a frog telling
what he knows
in language

we will fall asleep to.
Come morning, he's a souvenir,
a change purse for a tourist.

In a wash of early light,
rosy stacks of roofing tiles
are a displaced colony

of coral. *Where are we off to?*
cries the cactus, thrusting
from an old tire.

The horses take turns
sniffing their dole of table scraps
and look up.

A MOTHER'S TEN-SECOND HISTORY LESSON

Willows in the swollen Sorgue   roll the kayak the boy
is under long enough   for rosemary to bulk   into a hedge
breath moist   on the walls of Lascaux   to decompose
an oxide horse   its legs in the air all at once   making it sacred
the boy robed in current   the Pope dresses at Avignon
the Pope dresses at Rome   world and anti-world
of will he come up   in the time it takes Napoleon
to lose the Nile no   longer even than refusing to die
on Elba by increments   battles fought   dusty soldiers
carried over shoulders home   their legs in the air making them
wounded   there is no other way   to know history
a Pope fearing poison   eats alone under a canopy   listens
to the water rising   once so high it washed   all the bodies
from their crypts   even if   the boy should surface
you understand it matters   nothing that he's yours.

VERONA AS THE PAST

At dusk, the bridges of the Adige
were a study in perspective.
We stood on the longest bridge

between the color of yellow cherries
and the color of plums.
The cypress knew

what the sky had yet to find out.
Early evening, September,
and everything quickened.

A crowd gathered
where two men were going to fight—
life then so much like art.

They were young; the way they loved
people and things
tore at them.

And the sky darkened
before we knew where we would sleep.
It was the beginning of rain on stone.

A dog walked on the bias in the rain,
his head at eleven o'clock,
his tail end always at five.

AFTER THE FEAST

Not the silence that crosses me,
pressing a heavy thumb to my forehead,
but the napkins and cups

driven by the wind, like a long confession
in the mind of a priest walking home.
The stew is still warm. A day ago,

an hour ago, men drank rakí;
a groom swung his boot
high enough to brush a hand held

arrogantly high. Is scorn
any different than beauty?
How many times

will I come to this stone table
after all that will have happened.
Like a child that sleeps with its hands in the air,

how often to the litter and bones
will I return, expectant?
If the stones could only hear me!

If the ragged juniper could only hear,
or the donkey pressed close to its shade
as if to the body's last pleasure.

MONK KILLED BY TRACTOR IN BID TO DODGE POLICE

It was dark; he'd been driving
with his lights out to baffle the cops
who had cordoned off the monastery
he and the excommunicated brothers
refused to give up. During the siege,

he'd tried by night to reach
the olive grove or the artichokes,
the terraces needing to be plowed.
Or maybe he'd meant to use the tractor
as a tank. It overturned, crushing him.

In a holy war about differences
between archbishops and popes, deriving
from the Great Schism, precipitated
by the Crusades—which couldn't, in the end,
keep the Turks out of Constantinople—
he is only the most recent casualty.

Even Mehmet the Conqueror wept
when he saw how many had been killed
and the wholesale ruin of that beautiful city
his armies had sacked. At Hagia Sophia,
he dismounted then fell to his knees
and poured a handful of dirt over his turban.

PAGAN LITANY

The sea swells over the breakwater,
careers in heavy showers
across the harbor road
where salt pines
lie broken by the wind.
It's nearly dark by four P.M.

Through open doors, small markets
like gravesites surrender
a naïve collection of supplies:
ouzo, chocolate bars,
cigarettes and toys.

If we have souls, if we dare to think so
on a day like this, we play them
close to our bodies.
                    What gods there might be
won't hear us above the wind
or the tarp of the sky
lashed down. Days like this,

we demonstrate the simple
economies of our need

and bury our dead
with change in their pockets.

II

CONFESSIONS OF THE NATURAL WORLD

WAITING FOR TASSOS

(who said he would meet us here)

We don't give up.
The sun ticks across the mountain.
The white horse stands

saddled and loaded beside the stone shed,
not shifting its weight.
You don't die of waiting.

You eat another olive,
you count the stones,
your lips already bright from salt and sun.

Somewhere else,
Tassos is drinking an ouzo,
making love to somebody's daughter—

in one ear her tongue,
in the other the wearisome noise
of supplication: everywhere

men and women memorizing
the catechism of delay. On terraces,
in shops, heat-swollen, as far away as Romania,

we are living on locusts and honey,
we are holding out for friendship
as though we would be

the earth's forgotten—a beauty
to fall back on, like a final
incoherence before he comes.

PRIMER IN BLACK

With only black
I'll make you Crete—

with only the toil and sweat
of the olive. And the sea

that gleams like schist
beneath a thunderhead.

In the tall, cylindrical hat
of the priest, a blessing

will follow the goat—
the black one fate has singled out

to cross town in a pickup truck.
They'll offer you rakí

and sweets, little fruits
candied and sugared.

But the indolent flies
won't let you eat,

will circle your plate—
an annoying chorus

of the perfect
failing to happen.

Let them be. It's simple
in black—this rigid alphabet

at the hands of which you only
approximate yourself.

Like my friend who returned
to a place not his home

with black shoes
when what he wanted was black

shoe polish. There's precision
in grief, but joy

is not exactly what you meant.
Like him, you'll fall asleep

with your feet in the new
strange shoes, the more comfortable pair

perfectly good
and empty beside the bed.

REPORT FROM MY OWN BACKYARD

October's done its mischief here already.
As has the cat. There's a vole
spinning like a dervish
on the walk near my back door.

A missing foot? A wound? Anything
but ecstasy I can believe. When I box it
for transport to the neighbor's pines, its body
thumps the cardboard. Let's think of this
as a primer. My Own Backyard.
It's where I'm told I should begin.

And it's greedy for attention.
Always the chickadees; sometimes
the finches. I arrange the errant hose
in the tidy coils of my mind.

The lawn chair on its side will gather snow.
I picture myself
going out with the sole purpose
of bringing that chair in. I should begin
in my own backyard,

where the plumbing
of the recently departed
boiler flails. There's no shame in devotion
to my little nation of stinks and groans,

this compost pile feeding skunks—
the hegemony of the hedge
on one side, the clear boundary
of my refusal to mow on the other.

I could die here, so convenient a plot.
I could wave my apron like a flag. Come home!

Come home! Leave others
to their yards and bones. Bury me
by the quid pro quo of the quince,
the shed's *don't-ask-me* shrug.

LANDSCAPE WITH A VERY FAT MAN, SEATED

Chicago Zoo, 2004

The man is alone but not extinct.
Not like a muse or a nude does he sit,

friendly planet in the concrete amphitheater.
Not by the rivers of Babylon is it November.

But here. You are here. The seal sleeps on a rock,
in the asset of her winter blubber.

Late afternoon, sky white, gates wide open.

Who can say if the man is in exile
from the tiny seats reservable everywhere?

In the neighborhood of the seal,
he bears resemblance. Though not having a neck

has never been the seal's salvation,
perhaps it is a comfort in these last days.

THE MOMENT: STONE FISH

I fell in love
with a fish of Parian marble.
I loved the torqued, heavy

curve of the tail, the present,
tense and flirting
with departure.

In the hot, white village,
the sky one blue,
I put language behind me,

a monk's knot
at the back of my head.
I grew a long beard

to catch what fell from my lips—
crumbs and bones, the slim
pickings of the moment.

And though I practiced
perpetual-eye,
mouth-round-with-wonder,

the fish would not have me.
I touched it once,
its marble cool and bald,

then knew, just as a lover does,
to take my hand away.
I hurried to the future

in words like wind-flaw
on the surface of deep water.
Now, where the sea leaves

weedy slaw behind it
on the sand, I throw whole days
like fish gut to the gulls.

CONFESSIONS OF THE NATURAL WORLD

Greece, 2003

It is winter and likely
that spring will mean war.
Not here, though who knows
what will happen now.
Each day we read the faces
of refugees in the news—
the rescued because the drowned
don't appear.
Like priests, we do nothing
the best we can:
we hear the confessions
of the wind and the rain—

the clementines falling
prematurely, the lemons this year
too small to cut.

At Livada
a dolphin washes up on the beach,
neatly pithed, stuffed with weeds.

And walking the streambed
at the bottom of the valley,
we find two sheep,
hobbled, that have fallen in,
dispelling the myth
of the good shepherd.

It's winter in the tin cans and back gardens
of houses, where red geraniums
linger, like decorated heroes
of a previous war.
In January, when the papery
bougainvillea let go,

rosemary takes heart and carries on—
purple blossoms
in spite of everything.

Beauty is a thumb in the mouth,
safety the warmth
of a heater in a small room
over the faint smell of propane.

It's winter, and acting
like an occupied country
comes easy once you know how.
After the south wind
we scavenge at Porto, after the north
at Kolimbithra, taking
whatever the sea coughs up:

chair legs, pallets, driftwood, trash.
When a sailboat used for smuggling
immigrants runs up on the rocks,
we burn its hundreds
of splintered boards, the sea salt
throwing a miserly assurance
of sparks.

For night maneuvers, the mind
requires no amphetamines.
All around this darkened planet,
invisible among cypress
and olive trees, in the desert
and the thorny maquis,
troops are moving.

I hear bombers overhead
on their way to Turkey. If it's only
the wind down from Exombourgo,
shifting to the south at three A.M.,
somewhere, someone lies listening
to what isn't the wind.

BEETLE

Why this panic
inside when the chapel door gave
so easily to the pressure of your hand?
Is it the sadness of icons—
their eyes on you
in the candled dark?

Or the sweet must of the air
like a well-groomed corpse?

Someone has laid out doilies and saved
these water bottles for oil.
Though you may be alone,
you're not wholly unseen.

Flee with your back
to those wide-awake faces.
Or keep an eye there and ease
toward the door.

Outside, just olive trees,
donkey skat. A beetle,
unswervingly black,
trundles across the rutted road.

No one asks you to believe
the intelligence of chitin, its chronic
dung-joy.

STORM COMING TO TORCELLO

Under the stone loggia, strangers wait
among strangers. Lightning flashes
in the direction of Burano.
                                        The skin pricks up,
sends its messengers to the interior.
The dark points of cypresses shift
like manic compass needles.
Remember when you thought
that everything could happen?
                                        Even the oldest
among us—smoking, pensive—quickens
to the far-off shrieks that become the bright
splash of slickers as children appear
running toward us, in their wet faces our own
extraordinary future.

DOGS AT THE TEMPLE OF THE OLYMPIAN ZEUS

Of the original one hundred
and four columns, only fifteen remain standing,
a sixteenth tumbled by a storm
in 1852 and left to lie
in a lovely row of discs.
The statues are gone, the megalithic Zeus
and Hadrian, pediments and friezes
saved from exhaust and acid rain
in a museum, or recycled
by a Turkish emperor. For figures
on this site, you have only my mother—
careful with her footing—
a pair of Germans posing
for the camera, and the dogs.

One dog is a mother herself.
For her someone has erected a cardboard roof
at a corner of the Roman baths—
a gesture especially touching, given
the Greek ambivalence toward animals.
Now all four tourists
stand ogling the puppies, as if sharing
some benevolent wish. We've seen
and tried to ignore the other dog,
the one closer to the temple.
"He'll have maggots," my mother said
as we passed a few minutes ago. On each of his ears
was a wound the size of a small marketplace,
which the flies had colonized in earnest.

I'd rather think of that sixteenth column
as toppled by no aggressor worse
than bad weather—give or take
a scavenger or two, who might have melted down
metal clamps for use as ammunition. I love to see

things go gracefully, the columns pitched
tall against their own ruin—
and how one lovely city dies
into the arms of another, albeit less lovely.
But the dog has shown up
as dazed and hungry as a prophet
in our midst. My mother
is reading from the brochure, something
about the dictator Peisistratos
and the energies of an unhappy people.
The Corinthian order
sounds like a religious sect,
or a type of column with Franciscan leanings.
But there are no monks
feeding sparrows, there are
no sparrows at all. My mother

is following the tides of history
that raised and lowered this temple,
centuries in each direction, and I'm studying
that slouching cardboard shack, good
for a day or two at best.
I'm back at the ancient Olympic Stadium,
where half an hour ago,
I watched overweight men in their fifties
lumber in to the finish
of a 10K race—failed proof that we're not
a civilization in decline.
Seeing burns on that dirty dog's ears,
I'm remembering the dirty bombs I read about
in the *Herald Tribune*—how you could carry one
in your coat pocket and, cutting it loose,
do in a neighborhood
the size of Soho or Lincoln Park.

Now the Germans have set off
for the Stoa of Attalos,
and my mother's looking really small
in capri pants over near Hadrian's Gate—
as helpless as I am in the cause for good.
Though I know their stone heads and hands
would have been broken off early on—
victors or vandals could have done
a thing like that—I wish just a few of the gods
had been left standing.

LITANY OF RESISTANCE

I am the sum of forgetting and neglect—
some days perhaps more
like one who resigns from the committee
in a rumpled shirt

than a small resistance movement
waving poems, my banners
of indolence.

Either way, mail goes unopened.
People I know lunch alone
because I never call.

I'm tired of even the kindliest lies.

In the village where I live, a pickup
trolls the streets, its bullhorn
hawking dishpans and carpets.
A woman sitting in a doorway
shows me, as I pass, the sores beneath
the bandage on one leg.

This much I know for sure. Each day
she lifts the bandage and I say hello—
the only thing I remember the word for.
I shake my head sadly and say it again
because it also means good-bye.

The truck with the loudspeaker
labors down the mountain.
The mountain drops silently to the sea.

There are no billboards,
no newspapers here.
At dinner I don't recall

a single episode from Caesar's *Gallic Wars.*
Even Latin I have forsaken

for a bowl of yellow-green pears,
for flies at their humble
revolutions.

WHAT THEY HAD COME FOR

It is no contest of strength or endurance.
The white butterfly flaps, like a pair of pillowcases
in a breeze, around the sparrow—
flaps fondly as if the world were all about
beauty or friendship. He hops as sparrows do—
hops, dancing, near her, isolate on the roof.
Of an overcast day, they are the soul.
Or she is the soul, in her white robes.
He, the body in monkish brown, levitates
like so, like so. He does not need to spread his wings
to devour her. One petal of her floats
gracefully above and away, as if she had merely
misunderstood this dancing
that seemed it was what they had come for.

III

METAPHOR AS PRAYER

METAPHOR AS PRAYER

Beneath the enameled
wings of the ladybug
I imagine the city of Beijing.
Early summer. Awnings open
on a street off Tiananmen Square.
Ash rises from an incinerator.

That each particle of the universe
is saturated with the rest—
all of it contained in a petal of the lobelia
dangling from my flowerbox—
was Emerson's idea.
The damage done the echinacea
last night by groundhogs
is the Russian steppe.
There's a Cossack in my roses.

So pruning, watering,
sprinkling cayenne,
I am Gorbachev in China
or Golda Meir negotiating
a difficult peace.

On the outskirts of Jerusalem,
a boy sleeps,
like the boy still sleeping
in the back room of my house.
The Oversoul
is the arrangement of limbs
they share, the sweet cure
of arms bent close to the face.

My chest ticks lazily.

The bomb does not go off—
car parked, driver asleep
in the late morning sun.
There's a holy day in my heart
in the heart of the terrorist.

REPORT FROM THE AFTERMATH

After a revolution there is a brief
period of bulletins
and confetti. There are dead women
in the arms of dead men;
there are men still with arms
in convoys headed back
to villages that are gone. Nobody knows where
things belong in the kitchens of the rich.

Before long it's hard to remember
those giddy first days
playing with the intercom
in the dictator's palace,
or how it was to be a teenager, even.

After a flood,
everything ripples,
wallboard and floorboards.
Living rooms become fertile.

After a hurricane, after divorce,
after the news of death, the nukes,
after great pain the formal feeling
gives way to rust or malice,
the pilfering of aid.

What if this is only a test:
after an illness
either brief or sustained,
a man is dying alone
in a rented room.
You're his son,
he shits himself,
he wanted it this way.

Think back.
I know. It's hard to remember
how it was in the long
quiet of that low pressure system
when you prayed you'd survive
whatever it was, then feared
it wouldn't come.
Was there ever a time
you thought he might have loved you?

THE HEART IS

a heavy woman
on a motorbike, testing the shocks,
a bus on a dark road,
one headlight out.

In the discrepancy between
daylight and moonlight
you leave the establishment,
counting your change.

The cows come home.

And if life goes on
like this for a while, well then?

At sea
a ferry strung with yellow lights
renders its service
all the way past until.

You watch from high above.
The passengers are reading
books you don't figure in,

saying to one another,
So home is where?

ELEGY FOR MY NOVEL

At first the ants come singly,
heads to the wall,
obedient like old sewing machines
in a back room in Piraeus.
They're an error
copied, a language dubbed.

Then they're socialists, the propaganda
of their own need. They post
invisible bills so by nighttime
they've smoked a trail down my wall.
A gang in black balaclavas
violates my bed. Or gods
in chitin drag: they try my pillow,
loll in the ephemera
of my lotions and oils, cart off
bits of skin for their reliquaries.

With a shoe or a book
I would stop their quotidian march,
but the work of ants
is to let you know how long
the story really is—that you'll fall asleep
not even halfway through.
After only a sentence or two,
after *Once.* That's why new waves of ants

emerge like second-graders
inventing the same old jokes:
forty thousand years of knock-knock
and Polacks we keep falling for
while the micro-hordes descend
from cracks above the door jambs.
Craven, they grow wings—
drop from the light fixture to the table

where I am laboring over
my novel. They work it
like a papery grave. Nubile as agents,
they flit and shift—it's a wonder
I didn't see them coming.
I'm not proud, but how I loved

the American innocent abroad.
She never wanted
the East German poet to die, even
when he set fire to the palace.

And old Dimitri,
and the woman who swam
halfway to Turkey in a dress
and one fin—they're surfacing
the way the bodies of friends
and loved ones turn up in wrong places—
on surgeons' tables, or in wooded areas
near the highway, tragic beyond
the call of any plot.

I never believed
in the promise of a New World, the Pilgrims,
never thought the founding fathers
loved me in their buckled shoes.
Maybe my heart was already breaking.

Now the ants are on my font—
all caught up in new wings
like the sussurous lips of children
pretending to read.

They're the Zen drone
of the lost self, they're Zem Zem

Shriners at the critics' parade,
troops on the rations of my failing

good will. And if I raise a fist to kill,
their touchy alphabet's already
leaving the page, like the fine line
between *insane* and *inane,*
histrionic and *history.*

FEAST

In the beginning

was thyme in a goat's mouth,
pink oleander by the sea.
Then we climbed the mountain
path and flayed the goat.

The priest broke bread.
The earth fell away.

Drinking to what
we did not understand,
we appeared to one another
in the mist.

THEORY OF AN IMPERSONAL GOD

I remember Souad almost drowning
this time to Schubert's *Ave Maria.*
        An operatic voice drifts above
where I sit on the terrace,

amid the laurel and the prickly pear.
                Why think of spirit
as air? More likely it is water—
the edgy blues
        in which the body floats or sinks.

        I do not know the swells
are taking her breath, the currents
I've only heard about
        not declaring themselves to me.
                I wave from shore, refreshed,
roughed up a little by the wind.
Maybe Souad isn't looking.

The voice of the soprano makes me distant
even from myself.
                Is that me
who turns from the water and runs
toward the dunes, hot sand caving

in over my feet?
        You could die of beauty.
        Which means that now I nurse an ouzo,
hear the cicadas in the terraced field.
        Metaphor is the luxury
                of *almost, not quite.*

You can die a death so literal
it makes a hole in the sea the shape of you.

And God doesn't bat an eyelash.
God who is nothing
like the flashing of eels
or the sea's interminable blue.

TIGERS

In the zoo yard in moonlight
two tigers are sleeping, spine to spine, each mirrored
by the other's lack of intention—the stretch of a forepaw,
the incline of a head. Their synchronous
yawns divide the earth into hemispheres: the great
continents of their backs, the Occident
and the Orient of their rumps. Tails twitch
a memory of differential happiness.

The corridor of their dream is papered in birch.
They sleep without lassitude—
quiet only as cities are quiet, lit and humming
beneath the breath—the repose of yang and yang.

If scholars, they're incestuous, referencing
only each other. No master text.
If words, we love them
for having heard them together.
When Blake said *Tyger! Tyger!* he invoked
just one cat—its bold graffiti suggesting a Maker
who had come like a vandal artist
then slipped back over the wall.
But these two in moonlight

are literalists. When I ask, *What immortal hand or eye?*
or say (of the worn grass) that night has read
the earth's Braille down to nothing,
they lie motionless where the grass is worn—
the great cages of their ribs falling and falling.

EVENING

Evening approaches
like a tall blind man
with a tiny woman
at his elbow they are making
their way down the steep
road toward town how beautifully
on the terraced
hillside they leave behind
things lie at their depths
the barrel for burning
beside the olive tree the stone
shed deep shadow
of the path and at the bottom
a russet-colored chicken
like a first cause
from which all things must rise.

She reaches up to hold
his arm (sun's
gone but there's this
dispensation of light
a space between
her old legs like an amphora
broken and restored
by her motion) how
beautifully things lie at their depths
the animals in the dovecote
on the hillside they tend
daily up and back
there were years
the meat hooks in the little house
collected only snow there were
Italians Germans Communists
the Colonels the years you couldn't
tell the sheep from the goats

and the white doves
flapped and rose
from the olive trees
to be shot all at once
anachronistic of a peace
so long ago no one
could remember.

Now they are old
his size applies to her progress
like a formula for the failing
light they are passed
by rental cars tourists she's so tiny
he could carry her
she must reach up to hold
his arm a Hercules
Cement truck rumbles
past sometimes the horrors
are swallowed up in moments
of beauty the memory
of a boy who's dead now

getting up in the night
to use the bathroom he would
have gone out through
the courtyard
would have seen the stars
or it's the way she said snow frosted
the great spikes of the yucca
this morning and wrapped
the dome of the church how in
a whiteout like that
the heart allows
a very small good

to compensate the blind
sweep of loss as when the man
and woman reach the harbor he
in a worn coat green hat
the lights that only she can see
beginning to come on.

LAST DAYS

Plenty of everything
these days to go around:
up from the drain, a handful of stars.
Two plates of small fish,
illegal this season.

The only ambition
is that of the cockroach,
the only discretion
ours. The cats, all in heat,
never tire of stating the obvious.

I am leaving. There is blue
jacaranda everywhere.
At the height of the season
I am cutting open the hours
like baby pears to reveal
this brutality at the center.

The waiter unbuttons
his white shirt briskly,
pulls until it billows
and the tails fly free,
then wipes the tables clean.

I am driving the mountain road
behind a farmer's pickup.
One cow rides supine in the back;
from the two who straddle her,
thrown on the curves, a rear
leg splays out over the bed.

I lay on the horn, follow at a distance.
I weep, I linger these last days,
knowing what I know.

On a jag of sadness
for things that happen once
or not at all, or that never should,
I am eating with the lights off,
the crush of jasmine
so sweet I can't think straight.

NIGHT IN VENICE: SUMMER

for E. D.

If death is at all
like friendship, then we'll go out
into the open dark of a city

where windows, lit gold,
hang like icons. High above the *campo,*
someone leaning from a window will see us

or hear our footsteps on stone.
We will not return
to empty chairs or obligations,

to rooms where the towels
mouth our names. Like children
pretending not to hear,

we will not go in. How much then
will we mean the things we say!
Tonight, on the steps of the *Salute,*

the air balmy and smelling of the sea,
we confess we'll change our lives—
and mean it in the way

the lemon bobbing past
in its rind of moonlight means
to be a universe.